ARTHUR RACKHAM
FAIRY TALES, FABLES, & FANTASY

OVER 100 PICTURES FOR YOU TO COLOR

Collected & Edited by **PAULA SPENCER**

A
MyColorArt™
Color & Draw Book

PICTURES

BY
ARTHUR RACKHAM

ARTHUR RACKHAM emerged in the early 1900's as one of the world's preeminent artists and illustrators, and his unique style quickly made him famous during his own lifetime. It is still easily recognized today, more than 75 years later. Born in England in 1867, he published his first illustrations in 1893 and worked steadily from then on until his death in 1939.

Acclaimed for his beautiful and detailed color paintings and the imaginative pen-and-ink drawings that he created for contemporary children's stories, he also illuminated many timeless classics of literature such as *Æsop's Fables*, *Alice's Adventures in Wonderland*, and *The Fairy Tales of the Brothers Grimm*, and there are selections from each of those books included in this book.

On the other hand, he occasionally depicted frighteningly grotesque and decidedly macabre scenes, such as the drawings included here from the artist's personally published edition of Edgar Allan Poe's *Tales of Mystery & Imagination*.

Whatever your own artistic interest and ability, we hope that you enjoy this wide-ranging collection of pictures for you to color that highlights the unique talent and fantastic imagination of Arthur Rackham.

❧

PAULA **S**PENCER, herself an accomplished graphic designer, has been a fan of Arthur Rackham's drawings and paintings for as long as she can remember. Though his popularity has waxed and waned over the years as fashions in illustration styles have changed, he experienced a major revival during the 1970's, when you could go to the art section of any bookstore and find numerous collections of his memorable illustrations. Perhaps, after seeing some of these drawings here, new fans will search out more of his work and discover his special gift for interpreting classic stories.

This page and the blank ones near the back of this book are good places to test your colors. Colored pencils are best, but you can also try Flair-type felt-tip pens, highlighters, various gel pens, or other quick-drying colored markers.

NOTE: It is suggested that you add one or two extra sheets of scrap paper behind the page that you're coloring to prevent any colors from leaking through to the next drawing, especially if you use very wet media (watercolors, Sharpie pens, Magic Markers, *etc.*). Also, make sure that you let the page that you're working on dry completely before closing the book.

This blank page is here to help protect the following illustrations from possible leak-through from your color tests.

PICTURES

SOME · CHILDREN ·

SOME
GROTESQUE

SOME
FAIRY TALES

& FANTASTIC

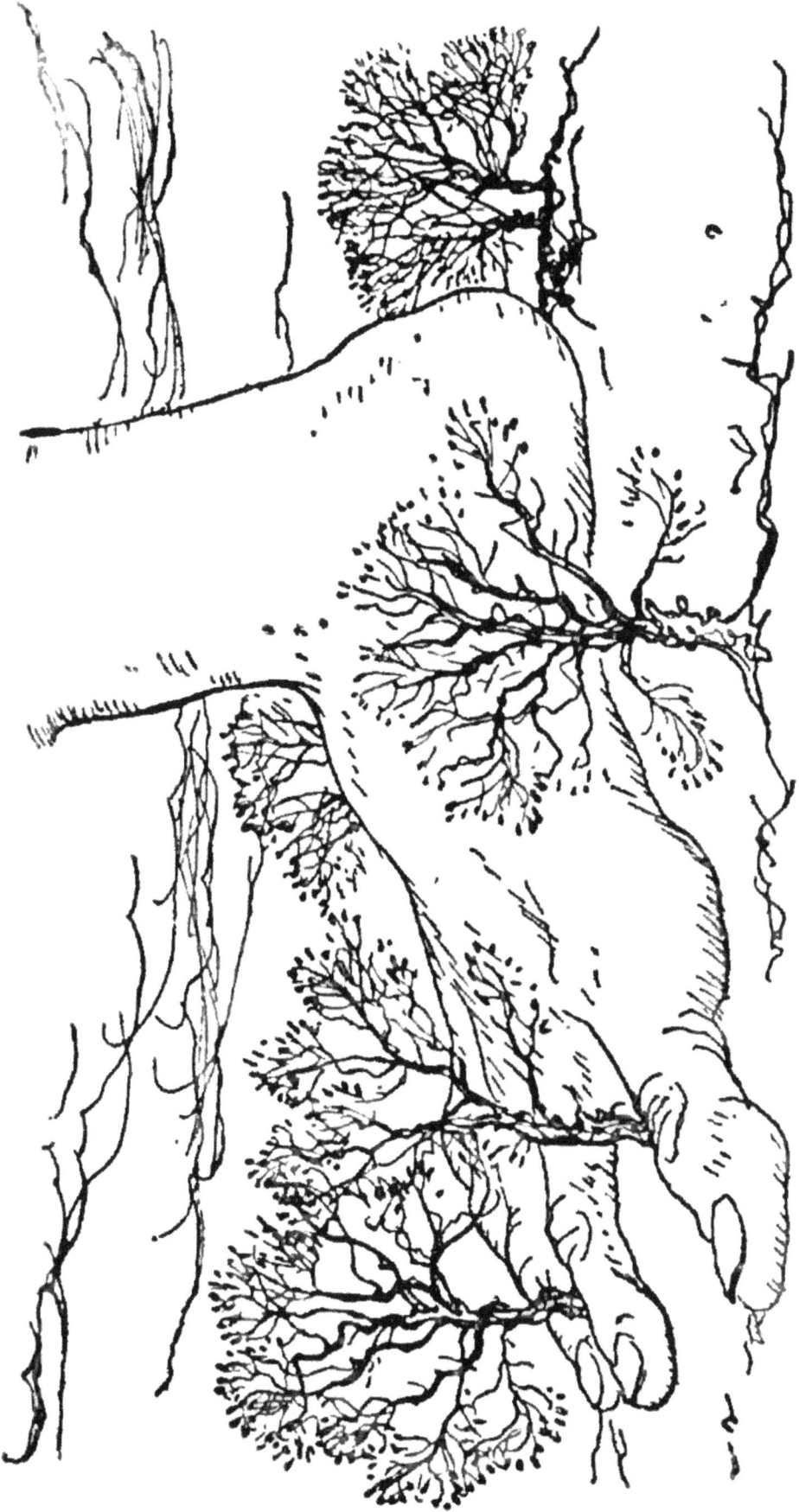

ÆSOP'S FABLES

A·NEW·TRANSLATION
BY·V·S·VERNON·JONES
WITH·AN·INTRODUCTION
BY·G·K·CHESTERTON
AND·ILLUSTRATIONS
BY·ARTHUR·RACKHAM

LONDON:WILLIAM·HEINEMANN
NEW·YORK:DOUBLEDAY·PAGE·&·Cº

Arthur Rackham, 1912

Arthur Rackham 1912

Arthur Rackham 1912

Arthur Rackham. 1912

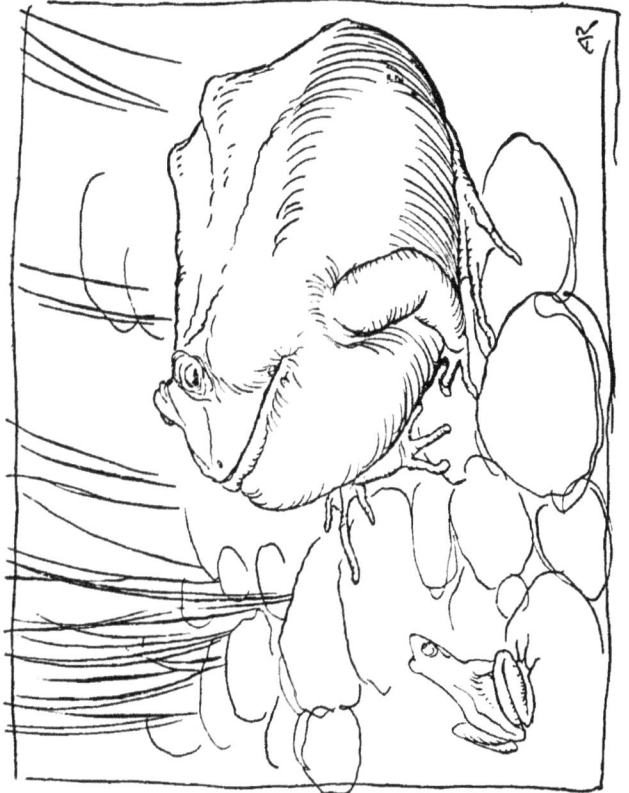

ALICE'S·ADVENTURES IN·WONDERLAND BY·LEWIS·CARROLL ILLUSTRATED·BY ARTHUR·RACKHAM

LONDON · WILLIAM · HEINEMANN
NEW · YORK · DOUBLEDAY · PAGE · & · Cº

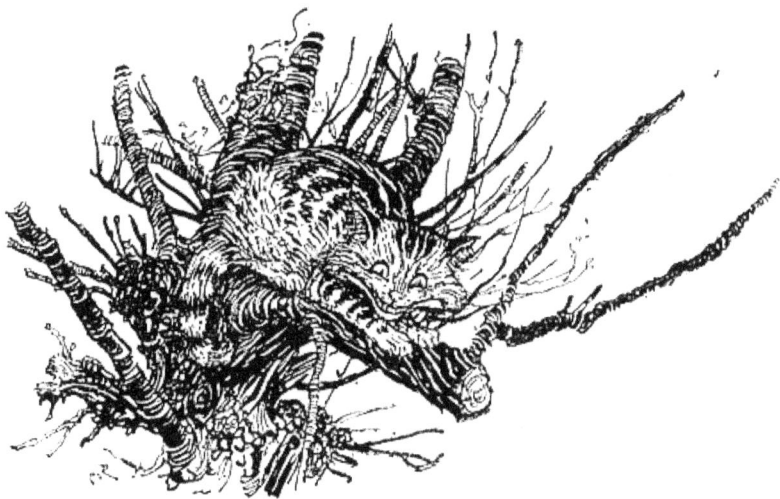

The Fairy Tales of the Brothers Grimm

Illustrated by
Arthur Rackham

Translated by
M^{rs}· Edgar Lucas

Arthur Rackham

The Golden Bird

Tales of Mystery & Imagination

By Edgar Allan Poe

Illustrated by Arthur Rackham

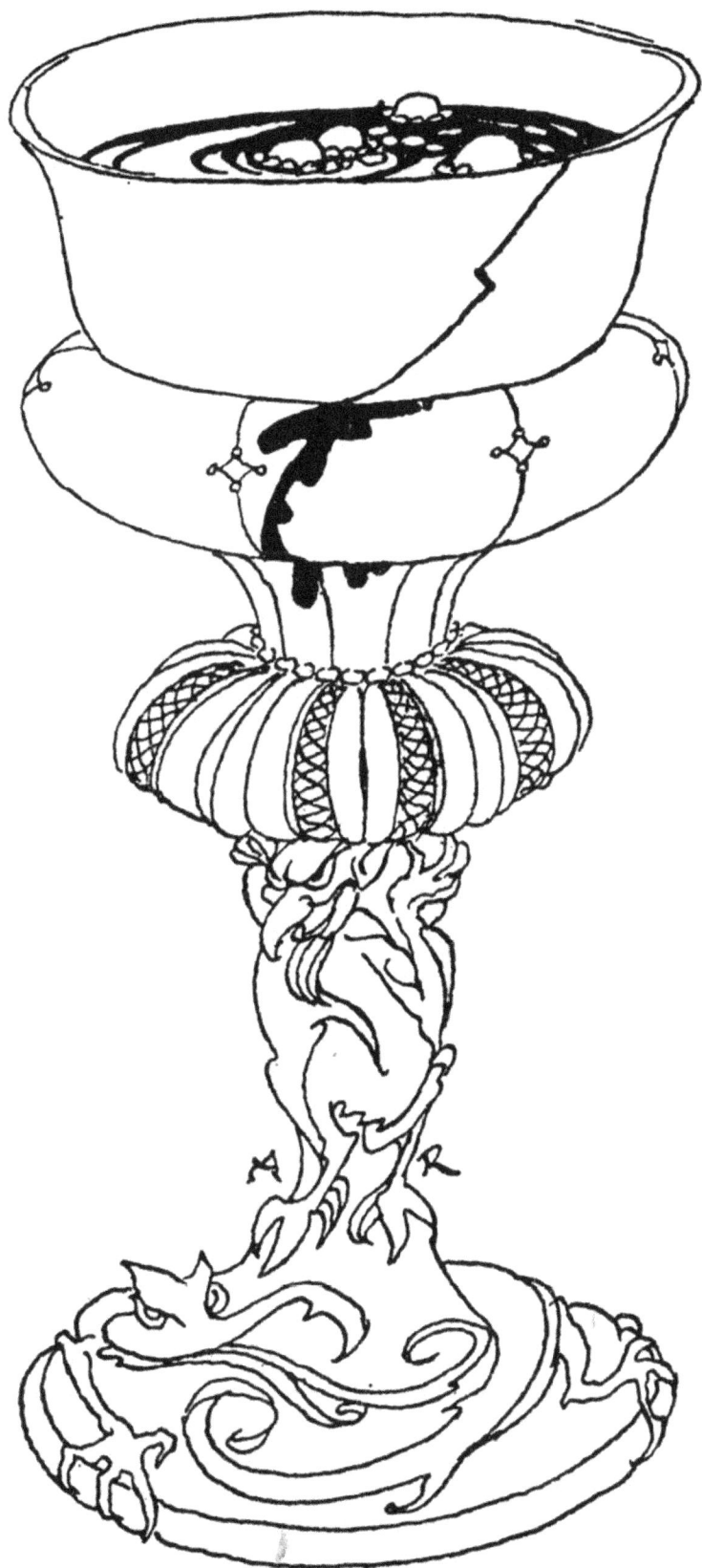

This is another page upon which you may test your colors.

Copyright © 2016 Gallant Press
Post Office Box 1
Oakfield, New York 14125

www.mycolorart.com

A
MyColorArt™
Color & Draw Book

www.ingramcontent.com/pod-product-compliance
Lightning Source LLC
Chambersburg PA
CBHW082326040426
42445CB00027B/1901